All-Time Favorite Chicken & Fish

simple stir-fries 2

Pull out your wok or skillet and make a sensational stir-fry for dinner tonight.

easy weeknight meals 12

Discover simple, satisfying choices that give new meaning (and taste) to weeknight fare.

savory grilled favorites 24

Fire up the grill and enjoy exciting new recipes for chicken, fish, and seafood.

fun family dinners 36

Enjoy time with your family—and a great meal. Choose a no-fuss recipe made with family-favorite ingredients.

metric cooking hints 46

index 48

The Better Your Home® Series
A collection of home-and-family publications from the publishers of *Better Homes and Gardens®* magazine.

ISBN: 0-696-23230-8

Pictured on the cover: Jalapeno and Basil-Glazed Chicken (see recipe, page 25)

simple
stir-fries

asian primavera stir-fry

Fettuccine, ginger, and sugar snap peas come together with chicken and dried mushrooms for a satisfying meal that delivers on taste and nutrition.

Start to finish: 30 minutes

- 1 ounce dried shiitake mushrooms
- 1 tablespoon cornstarch
- 6 ounces dried fettuccine
- 12 ounces skinless, boneless chicken breast halves
- 2 tablespoons dry sherry
- 2 tablespoons light soy sauce
- 1 tablespoon grated fresh ginger
- 2 cloves garlic, minced
- Nonstick cooking spray
- 8 ounces tiny whole carrots with tops (about 12), trimmed
- 1 cup sugar snap peas (strings and tips removed)
- 4 green onions, bias-sliced into 1-inch pieces
- Green onion strips (optional)

1. Combine dried mushrooms and 1 cup warm water; let stand for 15 minutes. Drain mushrooms, squeezing out excess liquid; reserve liquid. Slice caps; discard stems. For sauce, stir cornstarch into reserved mushroom liquid. Set aside.

2. Meanwhile, cook pasta according to package directions; drain. Cut chicken into bite-size pieces. Stir together chicken, sherry, soy sauce, ginger, and garlic.

3. Coat a wok or large skillet with cooking spray. Heat over medium-high heat. Stir-fry carrots and sugar snap peas in hot wok for 3 to 4 minutes or until crisp-tender. Add sliced green onions; stir-fry for 1 minute more. Remove vegetables.

4. Add chicken mixture to wok. Stir-fry for 2 to 3 minutes or until chicken is no longer pink. Push from center. Stir sauce. Add to center. Cook and stir until thickened and bubbly. Return cooked vegetables. Add mushrooms and cooked pasta. Stir all ingredients together. Cook and stir about 1 minute or until heated through. Serve immediately. If desired, garnish with green onion strips. Makes 4 servings.

Nutrition facts per serving: 333 cal., 3 g total fat (1 g sat. fat), 45 mg chol., 324 mg sodium, 48 g carbo., 25 g pro.

chicken, long bean, and tomato stir-fry

Aptly named Chinese long beans may be the produce understatement of the decade. Averaging 1½ feet long, they go the extra yard to bring meaty flavor and crunch to stir-fries and other dishes.

Start to finish: 30 minutes

- **6** ounces dried wide rice noodles or egg noodles
- **12** ounces skinless, boneless chicken breast halves
- **1** teaspoon Cajun seasoning or other spicy seasoning blend
- **4** teaspoons cooking oil
- **2** cloves garlic, minced
- **1** pound Chinese long beans or whole green beans, cut into 3-inch pieces
- **¼** cup water
- **2** medium tomatoes, cut into thin wedges
- **2** tablespoons raspberry vinegar

1. In a saucepan cook rice noodles in boiling, lightly salted water for 3 to 5 minutes or until noodles are tender. (Or, cook egg noodles according to package directions.) Drain. Return to saucepan; cover and keep warm.

2. Meanwhile, cut chicken into thin bite-size strips. Toss chicken with Cajun seasoning. Set aside.

3. Pour 2 teaspoons of the cooking oil into a large skillet. Heat over medium-high heat. Stir-fry garlic in hot oil for 15 seconds. Add beans; stir-fry for 2 minutes. Carefully add water to skillet; reduce heat to low. Cover and simmer for 6 to 8 minutes or until beans are crisp-tender. Remove beans from skillet.

4. Add the remaining oil to skillet. Add chicken; stir-fry for 2 to 3 minutes or until chicken is no longer pink. Return cooked beans to skillet. Stir in tomatoes and vinegar. Cook and stir until heated through. Serve immediately over hot cooked noodles. Makes 4 servings.

Nutrition facts per serving: 381 cal., 8 g total fat (1 g sat. fat), 45 mg chol., 334 mg sodium, 54 g carbo., 25 g pro.

easy sweet and sour chicken

Skip the hassle of deep-frying chicken pieces—use this nontraditional stir-fry recipe and start with frozen chicken chunks instead.

Start to finish: 30 minutes

- **1** 10-ounce package frozen cooked, breaded chicken breast chunks
- **1½** cups instant rice
- **1** 8-ounce can pineapple tidbits (juice pack)
- **1** large red or green sweet pepper, cut into 1-inch pieces
- **¼** cup red wine vinegar or vinegar
- **3** tablespoons sugar
- **2** tablespoons cornstarch
- **2** tablespoons soy sauce
- **½** teaspoon instant chicken bouillon granules
- **1** 8-ounce can sliced water chestnuts, drained
- Fresh parsley sprigs (optional)

1. Bake frozen chicken chunks according to package directions. Prepare uncooked rice according to package directions.

2. Meanwhile, drain pineapple, reserving juice. Add enough water to reserved juice to measure 1½ cups. Pour pineapple juice mixture into a medium saucepan. Add sweet pepper. Bring to boiling; reduce heat. Cover and simmer for 1 to 2 minutes or until pepper is crisp-tender.

3. In a small bowl stir together vinegar, sugar, cornstarch, soy sauce, and chicken bouillon granules. Stir into sweet pepper mixture. Cook and stir until thickened and bubbly. Cook and stir for 2 minutes more. Gently stir in chicken chunks, pineapple tidbits, and water chestnuts. Cook and stir until heated through.

4. Serve immediately over hot cooked rice. If desired, garnish with parsley sprigs. Makes 4 servings.

Nutrition facts per serving: 434 cal., 10 g total fat (1 g sat. fat), 67 mg chol., 1,142 mg sodium, 68 g carbo., 19 g pro.

shrimp in garlic sauce

Stir-fry the succulent shrimp just until they turn opaque. Overcooking toughens them.

Start to finish: 30 minutes

- 1½ cups instant rice
- ½ cup chicken broth
- 1½ teaspoons cornstarch
- 2 tablespoons margarine or butter
- 1 medium red sweet pepper, cut into thin strips
- 1 medium green sweet pepper, cut into thin strips
- 1 small onion, cut into thin wedges
- 2 to 3 teaspoons bottled minced garlic
- 1 12-ounce package frozen, peeled and deveined shrimp, thawed
- 2 tablespoons snipped fresh parsley

1. Prepare uncooked rice according to package directions. For sauce, in a small bowl stir together chicken broth and cornstarch. Set aside.

2. Add 1 tablespoon of the margarine to a wok or large skillet. Heat over medium-high heat. Stir-fry red and green sweet pepper, onion, and garlic in the hot margarine about 3 minutes or until vegetables are crisp-tender. Remove the vegetables from wok.

3. Add remaining 1 tablespoon margarine to wok. Add shrimp; stir-fry for 2 to 3 minutes or until shrimp turn opaque. Push shrimp from center of wok. Stir sauce. Add sauce to center of wok. Cook and stir until thickened and bubbly.

4. Return cooked vegetables to wok. Stir all ingredients together to coat with sauce. Cook and stir about 1 minute or until heated through. Stir snipped parsley into hot cooked rice. Immediately serve the shrimp mixture over rice mixture. Makes 4 servings.

Nutrition facts per serving: 285 cal., 7 g total fat (1 g sat. fat), 131 mg chol., 453 mg sodium, 37 g carbo., 18 g pro.

no-chop scallop stir-fry

Scallops are available in two sizes. Bay scallops measure about ½ inch in diameter and sea scallops about 1½ inches. Both are delicious in this easy stir-fry, but cut the large scallops in half before cooking.

Start to finish: 25 minutes

- **8** ounces dried Chinese egg noodles or vermicelli, broken into 3- to 4-inch pieces
- **12** ounces fresh bay or sea scallops
- **¼** cup soy sauce
- **3** tablespoons dry sherry or apple juice
- **½** teaspoon ground ginger
- **1** tablespoon cooking oil
- **1½** teaspoons bottled minced garlic
- **2** cups loose-pack frozen stir-fry vegetables

1. In a large saucepan cook egg noodles in boiling water for 3 to 4 minutes or until tender. (Or, cook vermicelli according to package directions.) Drain. Return to saucepan; cover and keep warm.

2. Meanwhile, rinse scallops; pat dry with paper towels. Cut sea scallops in half. Set aside. For sauce, in a small bowl stir together soy sauce, sherry, and ginger.

3. Pour cooking oil into a wok or large skillet. (If necessary, add more oil during cooking.) Heat over medium-high heat. Stir-fry garlic in hot oil for 15 seconds. Add frozen vegetables; stir-fry for 2 to 3 minutes or until crisp-tender. Remove vegetables from wok.

4. Add scallops to wok. Stir-fry for 1 to 2 minutes or until scallops turn opaque. Push scallops from center of wok. Add sauce to center. Return cooked vegetables to wok; add cooked noodles. Toss all ingredients together to coat with sauce. Serve immediately. Makes 4 servings.

Nutrition facts per serving: 285 cal., 6 g total fat (1 g sat. fat), 62 mg chol., 1,178 mg sodium, 37 g carbo., 18 g pro.

easy
weeknight
meals

margarita chicken

For soft, warm flour tortillas, stack and wrap them in foil and heat in a 350° F oven about 10 minutes. Or, microwave tortillas, covered, on 100% power (high) for 30 to 45 seconds.

Prep: 15 minutes Broil: 12 minutes

- ½ teaspoon finely shredded lime peel
- ¼ cup lime juice
- 2 tablespoons tequila
- 2 tablespoons honey
- 1 tablespoon cooking oil
- 2 teaspoons cornstarch
- ¼ teaspoon garlic salt
- ¼ teaspoon coarsely ground black pepper
- 4 skinless, boneless chicken breast halves (about 1 pound total)
- Lime slices, halved (optional)
- 4 flour tortillas, warmed
- 1 medium tomato, cut into 8 wedges
- 1 medium avocado, seeded, peeled, and cut up

1. For glaze, in a small saucepan stir together lime peel, lime juice, tequila, honey, cooking oil, cornstarch, garlic salt, and pepper. Cook and stir over medium heat until thickened and bubbly. Cook and stir for 2 minutes more. Remove from heat.

2. Place chicken on the unheated rack of a broiler pan. Broil 4 to 5 inches from the heat for 12 to 15 minutes or until chicken is no longer pink (170° F), turning once halfway through broiling and brushing with some of the glaze the last 5 minutes.

3. Drizzle chicken with the remaining glaze. If desired, garnish with lime slices. Serve chicken with tortillas, tomato, and avocado. Makes 4 servings.

Nutrition facts per serving: 415 cal., 16 g total fat (3 g sat. fat), 59 mg chol., 356 mg sodium, 39 g carbo., 26 g pro.

so-easy chicken breasts

Feel good about serving this tasty chicken and wild rice dish to your family. With a fruit salad on the side, you'll be providing nutritious foods from every food group.

Start to finish: 30 minutes

- 1 6-ounce package long grain and wild rice mix
- ¼ cup thinly sliced green onions
- 1 cup broccoli florets
- 4 Italian-style or butter-garlic marinated boneless chicken breast halves (about 1 pound total)
- 2 teaspoons olive oil
- 1 medium tomato, thinly sliced and halved
- ¾ cup shredded mozzarella cheese (3 ounces)

1. Prepare rice mix according to package directions, adding green onions the last 5 minutes of cooking. Meanwhile, in a covered small saucepan cook broccoli in a small amount of boiling water about 3 minutes or until crisp-tender; drain. Return to saucepan; cover and keep warm.

2. In a large skillet cook marinated chicken in hot oil over medium heat for 8 to 10 minutes or until chicken is no longer pink (170° F), turning once.

3. Overlap tomato slices on top of chicken. Top with broccoli and sprinkle with mozzarella cheese. Serve chicken on top of hot cooked rice mix. Makes 4 servings.

Nutrition facts per serving: 377 cal., 12 g total fat (4 g sat. fat), 22 mg chol., 1,532 mg sodium, 38 g carbo., 31 g pro.

keys-style citrus chicken

The tropical-island-inspired cooking of the Florida Keys draws on the bes of both worlds. Here, it combines fresh Florida citrus with the Caribbea penchant for fiery peppers. Soak up the delicious juice with hot rice.

Start to finish: 20 minutes

- 4 skinless, boneless chicken breast halves (about 1 pound total)
- 2 or 3 cloves garlic, thinly sliced
- 1 tablespoon butter or margarine
- 1 teaspoon finely shredded lime peel
- 2 tablespoons lime juice
- ¼ teaspoon ground ginger
- ⅛ teaspoon crushed red pepper
- 1 orange
- Hot cooked rice (optional)
- Lime wedges (optional)

1. In a large skillet cook chicken and garlic in hot butter over medium heat for 8 to 10 minutes or until chicken is no longer pink (170° F), turning chicken once and stirring garlic occasionally.

2. Meanwhile, in a small bowl combine lime peel, lime juice, ginger, and crushed red pepper. Set aside. Peel orange. Reserving juice, cut orange in half lengthwise, then cut crosswise into slices. Add any reserved orange juice and the lime juice mixture to skillet. Place orange slices on top of chicken. Cover and cook for 1 to 2 minutes or until heated through.

3. To serve, spoon any reserved drippings over the chicken. If desired, serve with hot cooked rice and garnish with lime wedges. Makes 4 servings.

Nutrition facts per serving: 167 cal., 6 g total fat (3 g sat. fat), 67 mg chol., 84 mg sodium, 5 g carbo., 22 g pro.

mustard-topped salmon

Delicious on salmon, the mustard topping also perks up any broiled fish such as orange roughy, red snapper, cod, or halibut.

Start to finish: 20 minutes

- **1** pound fresh salmon fillets (with skin)
- **2** tablespoons mayonnaise, salad dressing, dairy sour cream, or plain yogurt
- **1** tablespoon Dijon-style mustard
- **1** teaspoon lemon-pepper seasoning

1. Rinse fish; pat dry with paper towels. Cut fish into 4 serving-size pieces. Measure thickness of fish. Place fish, skin sides down, on the greased unheated rack of a broiler pan, turning under any thin edges. Broil about 4 inches from the heat for 4 to 6 minutes per ½-inch thickness of fish or until fish flakes easily when tested with a fork.

2. Meanwhile, in a small bowl stir together the mayonnaise, mustard, and lemon-pepper seasoning. Spread mustard mixture over fish. Broil for 1 to 2 minutes more or until mustard mixture is lightly browned. Makes 4 servings.

Nutrition facts per serving: 159 cal., 10 g total fat (2 g sat. fat), 24 mg chol., 473 mg sodium, 1 g carbo., 17 g pro.

spicy fillets with toasted pecans

The crispy coating and toasted pecans earmark this pan-fried fish as a sample of Southern-style cooking.

Start to finish: 25 minutes

1. Rinse fish; pat dry with paper towels. Cut fish into 4 serving-size pieces. Measure thickness of fish. Set aside.

2. In a shallow dish stir together flour, cornmeal, chili powder, and garlic salt. Dip fish into flour mixture, turning to coat.

3. In a 12-inch skillet melt 2 tablespoons of the margarine over medium heat. Cook fish in hot margarine for 4 to 6 minutes per ½-inch thickness of fish or until fish flakes easily when tested with a fork and coating is golden brown, turning once. Remove fish from skillet; cover and keep warm.

4. In the same skillet melt the remaining 1 tablespoon margarine over medium heat. Add pecans; cook and stir for 3 to 5 minutes or until lightly toasted. Stir in lemon juice and red pepper. Drizzle the pecan mixture over fish. Makes 4 servings.

Nutrition facts per serving: 267 cal., 14 g total fat (2 g sat. fat), 45 mg chol., 407 mg sodium, 11 g carbo., 24 g pro.

1 pound fresh firm-textured fish fillets (such as catfish, pike, lake trout, or orange roughy)

¼ cup all-purpose flour

2 tablespoons cornmeal

1 teaspoon chili powder

½ teaspoon garlic salt

3 tablespoons margarine or butter

¼ cup broken pecans

1 tablespoon lemon juice

⅛ teaspoon ground red pepper

easy salmon pasta

To save time, we cook the pasta and vegetables together in the same pan.

Start to finish: 30 minutes

- **2** cups loose-pack frozen mixed vegetables or one 10-ounce package frozen mixed vegetables
- **1½** cups dried corkscrew pasta
- **¼** cup sliced green onions
- **1** 11-ounce can condensed cheddar cheese soup
- **½** cup milk
- **½** teaspoon dried dill
- **¼** teaspoon dry mustard
- **⅛** teaspoon black pepper
- **2** 6-ounce cans skinless, boneless salmon or tuna, drained
- Fresh dill (optional)

1. In a large saucepan cook the frozen mixed vegetables, pasta, and green onions in a large amount of boiling water for 10 to 12 minutes or just until pasta is tender. Drain.

2. Stir soup, milk, dried dill, mustard, and pepper into pasta mixture. Gently fold in salmon. Cook over low heat until heated through, stirring occasionally. If desired, garnish with fresh dill. Makes 5 servings.

Nutrition facts per serving: 347 cal., 9 g total fat (4 g sat. fat), 56 mg chol., 827 mg sodium, 41 g carbo., 22 g pro.

savory
grilled
favorites

jalapeño and basil-glazed chicken

Basil and jalapeño? Sure! They marry perfectly brushed on this red-pepper-rubbed chicken.

Prep: 15 minutes Grill: 50 minutes

- **2** whole chicken breasts (about 2 pounds total), halved lengthwise
- **1** tablespoon olive oil
- **1** clove garlic, minced
- **¼** teaspoon salt
- **¼** teaspoon ground red pepper
- **½** cup jalapeño pepper jelly
- **2** tablespoons snipped fresh basil
- **1** tablespoon lime juice

1. If desired, remove skin from chicken. For rub, in a small bowl combine olive oil, garlic, salt, and ground red pepper. Spoon rub evenly over chicken; rub in with your fingers.

2. For sauce, in a small saucepan combine jalapeño jelly, basil, and lime juice. Cook and stir over low heat until jelly is melted. Remove from heat.

3. In a grill with a cover arrange medium-hot coals around a drip pan. Test for medium heat above the pan. Place chicken, bone sides up, on grill rack over drip pan. Cover and grill for 50 to 60 minutes or until chicken is no longer pink (170° F), turning once halfway through grilling and brushing with some of the sauce the last 5 minutes.

4. To serve, reheat and pass the remaining sauce with chicken. Makes 4 servings.

Nutrition facts per serving: 377 cal., 13 g total fat (3 g sat. fat), 104 mg chol., 226 mg sodium, 27 g carbo., 37 g pro.

ruby-glazed chicken breasts

These chicken breasts have such a rich flavor from the currant and apple glaze that you'd never guess they're low in fat.

Prep: 10 minutes Grill: 35 minutes

- **⅓** cup apple juice
- **3** tablespoons currant jelly
- **1** teaspoon cornstarch
- **¼** teaspoon salt
- **⅛** teaspoon dried marjoram, crushed
- **3** whole chicken breasts (about 2¼ pounds total), halved lengthwise

1. For sauce, in a small saucepan combine apple juice, currant jelly, cornstarch, and salt. Cook and stir over medium heat until thickened and bubbly. Cook and stir for 2 minutes more. Remove from heat. Stir in marjoram. If desired, remove skin from chicken.

2. Place chicken, bone sides up, on the rack of an uncovered grill directly over medium coals. Grill for 35 to 40 minutes or until chicken is no longer pink (170° F), turning and brushing once with sauce halfway through grilling.

3. (Or, in a grill with a cover arrange medium-hot coals around a drip pan. Test for medium heat above the pan. Place chicken, bone sides down, on grill rack over drip pan. Cover and grill for 50 to 60 minutes, brushing occasionally with sauce the last 20 minutes of grilling.)

4. To serve, brush any remaining sauce over chicken. Makes 6 servings.

Nutrition facts per serving: 167 cal., 3 g total fat (1 g sat. fat), 69 mg chol., 150 mg sodium, 9 g carbo., 25 g pro.

herbed chicken breasts with avocado relish

To transform this dish into a salad, slice the chicken breasts and arrange them on plates lined with shredded lettuce. Top with the avocado mixture for a chunky dressing and add some shredded Monterey Jack cheese.

Prep: 20 minutes Marinate: 2 hours
Grill: 12 minutes

- **6** skinless, boneless chicken breast halves (about 1½ pounds total)
- **¼** cup dry white wine
- **2** tablespoons olive oil
- **2** teaspoons snipped fresh tarragon or ¼ teaspoon dried tarragon, crushed
- **¼** teaspoon salt
- **2** avocados, seeded, peeled, and chopped
- **1** tomato, chopped
- **2** green onions, finely chopped
- **2** tablespoons seeded and finely chopped jalapeño peppers
- **1** tablespoon snipped fresh cilantro
- **1** tablespoon honey
- **1** tablespoon lemon juice
- **1** clove garlic, minced
- Lettuce leaves (optional)

1. Place chicken in a plastic bag set in a shallow dish. For marinade, combine wine, oil, tarragon, and salt. Pour over chicken; seal bag. Marinate in refrigerator for 2 to 24 hours, turning bag occasionally.

2. Meanwhile, for avocado relish, in a small bowl combine avocados, tomato, green onions, jalapeño peppers, cilantro, honey, lemon juice, and garlic; toss gently to combine. Cover and chill up to 2 hours.

3. Drain chicken, reserving marinade. Place the chicken on the rack of an uncovered grill directly over medium coals. Grill for 12 to 15 minutes or until chicken is no longer pink (170° F), turning and brushing once with marinade halfway through grilling.

4. Serve the grilled chicken with the avocado relish and, if desired, lettuce leaves. Makes 6 servings.

Nutrition facts per serving: 239 cal., 16 g total fat (1 g sat. fat), 50 mg chol., 130 mg sodium, 5 g carbo., 20 g pro.

caramelized salmon with citrus salsa

Fragrant and delicious, this do-ahead recipe is especially impressive because the orange-scented rub turns a rich golden brown during grilling.

Prep: 20 minutes Marinate: 8 hours
Grill: 14 minutes

- 1 1½-pound fresh or frozen salmon or halibut fillet (with skin), 1 inch thick
- 2 tablespoons sugar
- 1½ teaspoons finely shredded orange peel
- 1 teaspoon salt
- ¼ teaspoon black pepper
- 1 teaspoon finely shredded orange peel
- 2 oranges, peeled, sectioned, and coarsely chopped
- 1 cup chopped fresh pineapple or canned crushed pineapple, drained
- 2 tablespoons snipped fresh cilantro
- 1 tablespoon finely chopped shallot
- 1 fresh jalapeño pepper, seeded and finely chopped

1. Thaw fish, if frozen. Rinse fish; pat dry with paper towels. Place, skin side down, in a shallow dish. For rub, stir together sugar, the 1½ teaspoons orange peel, the salt, and black pepper. Sprinkle rub evenly over fish (not on skin side); rub in with your fingers. Cover and marinate in the refrigerator for 8 to 24 hours.

2. Meanwhile, for salsa, in a small bowl stir together the 1 teaspoon orange peel, the oranges, pineapple, cilantro, shallot, and jalapeño pepper. Cover and chill up to 24 hours. Drain fish, discarding liquid.

3. In a grill with a cover arrange medium-hot coals around a drip pan. Test for medium heat above the pan. Place fish, skin side down, on the greased grill rack over drip pan. Cover and grill for 14 to 18 minutes or until fish flakes easily when tested with a fork.

4. Cut fish into 4 serving-size pieces, cutting to but not through skin. Using a metal spatula, lift fish away from skin. Serve fish with salsa. Makes 4 servings.

Nutrition facts per serving: 258 cal., 6 g total fat (1 g sat. fat), 81 mg chol., 688 mg sodium, 20 g carbo., 32 g pro.

dilly salmon fillets

A quick, dill-infused, Dijon-flavored mayonnaise caps off these Scandinavian-style salmon fillets. For a built-in salad and extra freshness, serve them on a bed of shredded cucumber.

Start to finish: 35 minutes

- **1½** **pounds fresh skinless salmon fillets**
- **3** **tablespoons lemon juice**
- **2** **tablespoons snipped fresh dill**
- **2** **tablespoons mayonnaise or salad dressing**
- **2** **teaspoons Dijon-style mustard**
- **Dash freshly ground black pepper**

1. Rinse fish; pat dry with paper towels. Cut fish into 4 serving-size pieces. Place fish in a shallow dish. For marinade, in a small bowl combine lemon juice and 1 tablespoon of the dill. Pour over fish. Cover and marinate at room temperature for 10 minutes.

2. Meanwhile, in a small bowl stir together the remaining dill, the mayonnaise, Dijon mustard, and pepper. Set aside.

3. In a grill with a cover arrange medium-hot coals around a drip pan. Test for medium heat above the pan. Measure thickness of fish.

4. Place fish on the greased grill rack over drip pan. Cover and grill for 7 to 9 minutes per ½-inch thickness of fish or until fish flakes easily when tested with a fork, gently turning once and spreading with the mayonnaise mixture halfway through grilling. Makes 4 servings.

Nutrition facts per serving: 211 cal., 11 g total fat (2 g sat. fat), 35 mg chol., 204 mg sodium, 1 g carbo., 25 g pro.

grilled rosemary trout with lemon butter

Taste the delicious reason lemon and butter remain the timeless, classic accompaniments to fish! This recipe is so simple you'll want to keep it handy for your next fishing trip.

Prep: 15 minutes Grill: 6 minutes

- **4** teaspoons butter, softened
- **1** tablespoon finely chopped shallot or onion
- **1** teaspoon finely shredded lemon peel
- **2** fresh rainbow trout, pan dressed and boned (8 to 10 ounces each)
- **1** tablespoon snipped fresh rosemary
- **1** tablespoon lemon juice
- **2** teaspoons olive oil
- **2** medium tomatoes, halved crosswise
- **1** tablespoon snipped fresh parsley

1. In a small bowl stir together butter, half of the shallot, and the lemon peel; sprinkle with salt and black pepper. Set aside.

2. Rinse fish; pat dry with paper towels. Spread each fish open and place skin sides down. Rub the remaining shallot and the rosemary onto fish. Sprinkle with additional salt and black pepper and drizzle with lemon juice and olive oil.

3. Place fish, skin sides down, on the greased rack of an uncovered grill directly over medium coals. Grill for 6 to 8 minutes or until fish flakes easily when tested with a fork. Meanwhile, place tomatoes, cut sides up, on grill rack alongside fish; dot each with 1/4 teaspoon of the butter mixture. Grill tomatoes about 5 minutes or until heated through. Remove fish and tomatoes from grill.

4. Cut each fish in half lengthwise. In a small saucepan melt the remaining butter mixture; serve with fish and tomatoes. Sprinkle with parsley. Makes 4 servings.

Nutrition facts per serving: 206 cal., 10 g total fat (3 g sat. fat), 75 mg chol., 109 mg sodium, 4 g carbo., 24 g pro.

fun
family
dinners

chicken fingers with honey sauce

Serve these oven-fried chicken strips with your favorite barbecue sauce as a quick alternative to the honey sauce.

Prep: 15 minutes   Bake: 11 minutes

- **12** ounces skinless, boneless chicken breast halves
- **2** cups cornflakes, crushed
- **¼** teaspoon black pepper
- **2** egg whites, slightly beaten
- **1** tablespoon honey
- **¼** cup honey
- **4** teaspoons Dijon-style or prepared mustard
- **¼** teaspoon garlic powder

1. Preheat oven to 450° F. Cut chicken into ¾-inch-wide strips.

2. In a shallow bowl stir together crushed cornflakes and pepper. In a small bowl combine egg whites and the 1 tablespoon honey. Dip chicken strips into egg white mixture. Dip into cornflake mixture, turning to coat.

3. Place chicken strips in a single layer on a baking sheet. Bake for 11 to 13 minutes or until chicken is no longer pink.

4. Meanwhile, for sauce, in a small bowl stir together the ¼ cup honey, the mustard, and garlic powder. Serve the chicken strips with sauce. Makes 4 servings.

Nutrition facts per serving: 230 cal., 3 g total fat (1 g sat. fat), 45 mg chol., 275 mg sodium, 31 g carbo., 19 g pro.

chili powder nuggets with cilantro cream

Sliced summer tomatoes and cucumbers make a refreshing accompaniment to these gunpowder nuggets. Try them as a tasty appetizer too, but double the cilantro cream sauce for dipping.

Prep: 15 minutes   Bake: 8 minutes

- ¼ cup cornflake crumbs or fine dry bread crumbs
- 1 tablespoon chili powder
- ½ teaspoon black pepper
- ¼ teaspoon salt
- ¼ teaspoon ground red pepper
- 1 pound skinless, boneless chicken breast halves
- 2 tablespoons margarine or butter, melted
- ½ cup dairy sour cream
- 2 tablespoons snipped fresh cilantro

1. Preheat oven to 400° F. In a plastic bag combine cornflake crumbs, chili powder, black pepper, salt, and red pepper.

2. Cut chicken into 1-inch pieces. In a medium bowl combine chicken pieces and melted margarine; toss to coat. Place in bag with cornflake mixture. Seal bag and shake until chicken is well coated.

3. Lightly grease a baking sheet. Place chicken pieces in a single layer on prepared baking sheet. Bake for 8 to 10 minutes or until chicken is no longer pink, turning pieces once.

4. Meanwhile, for cilantro cream, in a small bowl stir together sour cream and cilantro. Serve the chicken pieces with cilantro cream. Makes 4 servings.

Nutrition facts per serving: 252 cal., 15 g total fat (6 g sat. fat), 72 mg chol., 324 mg sodium, 5 g carbo., 23 g pro.

pulled chicken sandwiches

Pull the meat from a store-bought rotisserie chicken, and make a dressing. How simple. Bread-and-butter pickles and a spicy-sweet sauce make this big sandwich a real hero.

Start to finish: 30 minutes

- **1** 1¾- to 2-pound purchased roasted chicken
- **1** medium onion, cut into ¼-inch slices
- **1** tablespoon olive oil
- **⅓** cup apple cider vinegar or white wine vinegar
- **½** cup tomato sauce
- **3** to 4 tablespoons seeded and finely chopped fresh red and/or green serrano chile peppers
- **2** tablespoons snipped fresh thyme
- **2** tablespoons molasses
- **2** tablespoons water
- **½** teaspoon salt
- **4** kaiser rolls or hamburger buns, split
- Bread-and-butter pickle slices or sweet pickle slices

1. Cut the meat from chicken, discarding skin and bones. Using 2 forks or your fingers, pull chicken into shreds. Set aside.

2. In a large skillet cook onion in hot oil over medium heat about 5 minutes or until tender, stirring occasionally to separate slices into rings. Add vinegar. Cook and stir for 1 minute more.

3. Stir in tomato sauce, serrano peppers, thyme, molasses, water, and salt. Bring to boiling. Add chicken, stirring to coat. Cook and stir until heated through. Serve the chicken mixture on rolls with pickle slices. Makes 6 servings.

Nutrition facts per serving: 445 cal., 12 g total fat (3 g sat. fat), 84 mg chol., 990 mg sodium, 51 g carbo., 33 g pro.

salmon shortcakes

The secret to tender salmon patties is to handle the mixture gently and cook only until browned.

Start to finish: 25 minutes

1. Prepare Herbed Mayonnaise; set aside.

2. In a medium bowl combine egg and mayonnaise; stir in bread crumbs and green onion. Add salmon; toss to combine. Shape salmon mixture into eight ½-inch-thick patties. In a large skillet melt margarine over medium heat. Cook patties in hot margarine about 9 minutes or just until browned, turning once.

3. Split biscuits. Place 2 salmon patties on the bottom of each biscuit. Spoon on Herbed Mayonnaise; replace biscuit tops. Makes 4 servings.

Herbed Mayonnaise: In a small bowl stir together ¼ cup mayonnaise or salad dressing, 1 tablespoon snipped fresh dill, and 1 tablespoon milk. Stir in enough additional milk to make the mixture of drizzling consistency.

Nutrition facts per serving: 528 cal., 37 g total fat (8 g sat. fat), 121 mg chol., 1129 mg sodium, 23 g carbo., 26 g pro.

- **1 recipe Herbed Mayonnaise**
- **1 egg, beaten**
- **2 tablespoons mayonnaise or salad dressing**
- **¾ cup soft bread crumbs**
- **1 green onion, chopped**
- **1 14¾-ounce can salmon, drained, flaked, and skin and bones removed**
- **1 tablespoon margarine or butter**
- **4 purchased buttermilk biscuits, warmed, or one 10.8-ounce package refrigerated large flaky biscuits, baked**

oven-fried fish

Individually frozen fish fillets are perfect for busy cooks because you can cook them without thawing them first. In this easy recipe we toss them in seasoned crumbs and bake them in the oven.

Start to finish: 25 minutes

- **2** tablespoons margarine or butter
- **¾** cup cornflake crumbs
- **¾** teaspoon onion salt
- **¼** teaspoon black pepper
- **1** egg, beaten
- **1** tablespoon water
- **1** pound individually frozen fish fillets
- Tartar sauce

1. Preheat oven to 450° F. Place the margarine in a shallow baking pan. Place the pan in the oven for 2 to 3 minutes or until margarine is melted.

2. In a shallow dish stir together the cornflake crumbs, onion salt, and pepper. In another shallow dish combine the egg and water.

3. Measure thickness of fish. Dip frozen fish fillets into egg mixture. Dip into cornflake mixture, turning to coat. Place fish in the baking pan on top of the melted margarine.

4. Bake for 9 to 11 minutes per ½-inch thickness of fish or until fish flakes easily when tested with a fork. If desired, serve fish with tartar sauce. Makes 4 servings.

Nutrition facts per serving: 175 cal., 8 g total fat (2 g sat. fat), 96 mg chol., 414 mg sodium, 5 g carbo., 20 g pro.

Metric Cooking Hints

By making a few conversions, cooks in Canada, Australia, and the United Kingdom can use the recipes in this book with confidence. The charts on these pages provide a guide for converting measurements from the U.S. customary system, which is used throughout this book, to the imperial and metric systems. There also is a conversion table for oven temperatures to accommodate the differences in oven calibrations.

Volume and Weight: Americans traditionally use cup measures for liquid and solid ingredients. The chart (below) shows approximate imperial and metric equivalents. If you are accustomed to weighing solid ingredients, here are some helpful approximate equivalents.

- 1 cup butter, castor sugar, or rice = 8 ounces = about 230 grams
- 1 cup flour = 4 ounces = about 115 grams
- 1 cup icing sugar = 5 ounces = about 140 grams

Spoon measures are used for smaller amounts of ingredients. Although the size of the tablespoon varies slightly among countries, for practical purposes and for recipes in this book, a straight substitution is all that's necessary.

Measurements made using cups or spoons should be level, unless stated otherwise.

Product Differences: Most of the ingredients called for in the recipes in this book are available in English-speaking countries. However, some are known by different names. Here are some common American ingredients and their possible counterparts:

- Sugar is granulated or castor sugar.
- Powdered sugar is icing sugar.
- All-purpose flour is plain household flour or white flour. When self-rising flour is used in place of all-purpose flour in a recipe that calls for leavening, omit the leavening agent (baking soda or baking powder) and salt.
- Light-colored corn syrup is golden syrup.
- Cornstarch is cornflour.
- Baking soda is bicarbonate of soda.
- Vanilla is vanilla essence.
- Golden raisins are sultanas.

Useful Equivalents: U.S. = Canada/Australia/U.K.

Imperial / U.S.	Metric
½ ounce	15 g
1 ounce	25 g or 30 g
4 ounces (¼ pound)	115 g or 125 g
8 ounces (½ pound)	225 g or 250 g
16 ounces (1 pound)	450 g or 500 g
1¼ pounds	625 g
1½ pounds	750 g
2 pounds or 2¼ pounds	1,000 g or 1 Kg

Oven Temperature Equivalents

Fahrenheit Setting	Celsius Setting*	Gas Setting
300°F	150°C	Gas Mark 2 (very low)
325°F	160°C	Gas Mark 3 (low)
350°F	180°C	Gas Mark 4 (moderate)
375°F	190°C	Gas Mark 5 (moderate)
400°F	200°C	Gas Mark 6 (hot)
425°F	220°C	Gas Mark 7 (hot)
450°F	230°C	Gas Mark 8 (very hot)
475°F	240°C	Gas Mark 9 (very hot)
500°F	260°C	Gas Mark 10 (extremely hot)
Broil	Broil	Grill

*Electric and gas ovens may be calibrated using celsius. However, for an electric oven, increase celsius setting 10 to 20 degrees when cooking above 160°C. For convection or forced air ovens (gas or electric) lower the temperature setting 25°F/10°C when cooking at all heat levels.

Baking Pan Sizes

Imperial / U.S.	Metric
9×1½-inch round cake pan	22- or 23×4-cm (1.5 L)
9×1½-inch pie plate	22- or 23×4-cm (1 L)
8×8×2-inch square cake pan	20×5-cm (2 L)
9×9×2-inch square cake pan	22- or 23×4.5-cm (2.5 L)
11×7×1½-inch baking pan	28×17×4-cm (2 L)
2-quart rectangular baking pan	30×19×4.5-cm (3 L)
13×9×2-inch baking pan	34×22×4.5-cm (3.5 L)
15×10×1-inch jelly roll pan	40×25×2-cm
9×5×3-inch loaf pan	23×13×8-cm (2 L)
2-quart casserole	2 L

U.S. / Standard Metric Equivalents

⅛ teaspoon = 0.5 ml	¼ cup = 2 fluid ounces = 50 ml
¼ teaspoon = 1 ml	⅓ cup = 3 fluid ounces = 75 ml
½ teaspoon = 2 ml	½ cup = 4 fluid ounces = 125 ml
1 teaspoon = 5 ml	⅔ cup = 5 fluid ounces = 150 ml
1 tablespoon = 15 ml	¾ cup = 6 fluid ounces = 175 ml
2 tablespoons = 25 ml	1 cup = 8 fluid ounces = 250 ml
	2 cups = 1 pint = 500 ml
	1 quart = 1 litre

index

Asian Primavera Stir-Fry, 3
Avocados
  Herbed Chicken Breasts with Avocado Relish, 29
  Margarita Chicken, 13
Broccoli
  So-Easy Chicken Breasts, 25
Caramelized Salmon with Citrus Salsa, 31
Carrots
  Asian Primavera Stir-Fry, 3
Cheese
  So-Easy Chicken Breasts, 15
Chicken
  Asian Primavera Stir-Fry, 3
  Chicken Fingers with Honey Sauce, 37
  Chicken, Long Bean, and Tomato Stir-Fry, 5
  Chili Powder Nuggets with Cilantro Cream, 39
  Easy Sweet and Sour Chicken, 7
  Herbed Chicken Breasts with Avocado Relish, 29
  Jalapeño and Basil-Glazed Chicken, 25
  Keys-Style Citrus Chicken, 16
  Margarita Chicken, 13
  Pulled Chicken Sandwiches, 41
  Ruby-Glazed Chicken Breasts, 27
  So-Easy Chicken Breasts, 15
Chili Powder Nuggets with Cilantro Cream, 39
Dilly Salmon Fillets, 33
Easy Salmon Pasta, 23
Easy Sweet and Sour Chicken, 7
Fish
  Caramelized Salmon with Citrus Salsa, 31
  Dilly Salmon Fillets, 33
  Easy Salmon Pasta, 23
  Grilled Rosemary Trout with Lemon Butter, 35
  Mustard-Topped Salmon, 19
  Oven-Fried Fish, 45
  Salmon Shortcakes, 43
  Spicy Fillets with Toasted Pecans, 21
Herbed Chicken Breasts with Avocado Relish, 29
Jalapeño and Basil-Glazed Chicken, 25
Keys-Style Citrus Chicken, 16
Lemons
  Dilly Salmon Fillets, 33
  Grilled Rosemary Trout with Lemon Butter, 35
  Herbed Chicken Breasts with Avocado Relish, 29
  Spicy Fillets with Toasted Pecans, 21
Limes
  Jalapeño and Basil-Glazed Chicken, 25
  Keys-Style Citrus Chicken, 16
  Margarita Chicken, 13
Margarita Chicken, 13
Mustard-Topped Salmon, 19
No-Chop Scallop Stir-Fry, 11
Oranges
  Caramelized Salmon with Citrus Salsa, 31
  Keys-Style Citrus Chicken, 16
Oven-Fried Fish, 45
Pasta
  Asian Primavera Stir-Fry, 3
  Easy Salmon Pasta, 23
  No-Chop Scallop Stir-Fry, 11
Pineapple
  Caramelized Salmon with Citrus Salsa, 31
  Easy Sweet and Sour Chicken, 7
Pulled Chicken Sandwiches, 41
Ruby-Glazed Chicken Breasts, 27
Salmon Shortcakes, 43
Sandwiches
  Pulled Chicken Sandwiches, 41
Scallops
  No-Chop Scallop Stir-Fry, 11
Shrimp
Shrimp in Garlic Sauce, 9
So-Easy Chicken Breasts, 15
Spicy Fillets with Toasted Pecans, 21
Sweet and Sour Chicken, Easy, 7
Tomatoes
  Chicken, Long Bean, and Tomato Stir-Fry, 5
  Grilled Rosemary Trout with Lemon Butter, 35
  Herbed Chicken Breasts with Avocado Relish, 29
  Margarita Chicken, 13
  So-Easy Chicken Breasts, 15